THE BEST
OF
QUINCY SCOTT

To my friends in
Manzanita and Neah-kah-nie

Hughscott

Quincy Scott

THE BEST
OF
QUINCY SCOTT

A Picture Panorama
of the
Turbulent Depression and World War II Years
by the
Editorial Cartoonist
for the
Portland *Oregonian*
1931–1949

Introduced with commentaries
by
Hugh A. Scott

Oregon Historical Society
1980

In a book devoted to the work of a newspaper cartoonist, the natural selection for a type face is Times Roman, which was designed in 1931 by the distinguished English type designer Stanley Morison, as a newspaper face for the London *Times*. The version used in *The Best of Quincy Scott* is one of countless designs based on Morison's original face. The book was set by Harrison Typesetting, Inc., and printed by Durham & Downey, both Portland firms. The text paper is 70# and the cover stock is 80# Star-white Vicksburg smooth.

Designed by Bruce T. Hamilton

Original cartoons are in the collections of the University of Oregon Library, Eugene.

CONTENTS

FOREWORD

Where did the idea for this book — a selection of cartoons by Quincy Scott — originate?

The idea first occurred independently to my brother Allen (retired professor in chemistry from Oregon State University) and my sister, Mrs. J. Hudson (Dorothy Scott) Ballard, shortly after Quincy Scott's retirement from the *Oregonian* in 1949.

I suggested to dad at the time that he collaborate with me on a book of his cartoons. His response was negative; he had worked under pressure for so long that his reaction to retirement was a completely deflated ambition, and he did not want to start something that would require sustained concentration and hard work.

Looking back, it is just as well the book was not done then. Dad would have been a difficult collaborator; his involvement with his cartoons was so intense and personal that his selection would have varied considerably from that in hand, and he would have insisted upon certain points in the commentaries that might not have been wholly objective.

The idea resurfaced in the late fall of 1975, when the late Martin Schmitt, director of archives at the University of Oregon Library (where the Quincy Scott cartoons are housed), suggested that an anthology be done. He made the suggestion to my sister Dorothy, and she passed the idea along to me. I began work on a book to be called "Oregon: The Depression Years," to be based on research and interviews into the history of that period of Oregon, using Dad's cartoons as illustrations.

My work soon took a different direction, however. Lora Morgan, president of Morgan Press, conceived the notion of a book of Dad's cartoons, covering the full period of his service at the *Oregonian*. My sister referred Lora to me, and I was easily convinced that I should do the book as suggested.

There followed two trips to Eugene. During the first, I went through every cartoon dad had drawn, more than 6,000 in all. I made a "rough cut" to about 300 of the cartoons that were most apparently eligible for inclusion, using three criteria: technical excellence; aptness as an illustration of some problem of the day; and a certain balance among those that were local, regional, national or international in application.

Accompanied by my sister on a second trip, we selected ninety cartoons for final inclusion, and before we completed our work we tabulated the cartoons by the period in which they fell and the scope of their interest. By some coincidence, we came up with a good distribution without having to alter any selection.

Eventually, I took the manuscript to the Oregon Historical Society in Portland, which agreed to publish it, making another example of that institution's splendid publishing program. I am indebted to Thomas Vaughan and Bruce T. Hamilton at the Historical Society for their help in bringing this book to publication.

In preparing commentaries on the cartoons, my principal purpose has been to provide the historical, social and political background against which they should be viewed. While much of the subject matter was repetitive, especially that concerning Roosevelt and the New Deal, I saw no point in detailing the same information in several commentaries.

Dad was conservative, his cartoons reflected a conservative viewpoint, and I have felt that the commentaries should reinforce the points Dad was trying to make. Matters stated as fact, however, have either been researched or are based on my general knowledge of historical situations and incidents.

I wish to acknowledge the assistance of my sister, Dorothy Ballard, both in selecting the cartoons and editing the commentaries; by Martin Schmitt, Ed Kemp, and the staff in the Oregon Collections division of the University of Oregon Library, who not only made the original cartoons available but who carried the bulky cartoons back and forth from their niche in the stacks; to Thomas Vaughan and Bruce T. Hamilton of the Oregon Historical Society for their ideas and technical assistance in preparing materials and getting this book into print.

Two parting impressions. In looking over the 6,000 cartoons in two short days, I had an overwhelming feeling of topicality, the feeling that the problems of Quincy Scott's time were completely apposite to our own, and that the cartoons could be run today without change. The second impression was that very few of the entire set of cartoons were unworthy of inclusion in the anthology; ninety completely different cartoons could have been picked with little change in quality or breadth of coverage. In other words, the selection process was a tough job!

I hope the reader has as much enjoyment from glancing through this book of Quincy Scott's cartoons, perhaps recalling the temper of the times in which the cartoons appeared, as I had in assembling and writing about them.

Hugh A. Scott
1980

QUINCY SCOTT

Quincy Scott was a man in love with the West. Born and raised in the East, he did not get his first look at the West until 1907, when (with his new bride, the former Ella Beck Allen), he made a 2,500-mile horseback trip from St. Paul to Seattle, where Ella's mother lived. The trip is recorded in the recent book, *Horseback Honeymoon*, written by my sister, Mrs. Dorothy Scott Ballard.

This intimate introduction to the western United States had an important bearing on his cartoons. Scott loved horses, delighted in drawing them, and was an expert horseman. If he could find the slightest excuse for working a horse into a cartoon, he would do it. I have no doubt that he drew with the greatest enthusiasm his cartoon representing the vast Columbia River as the thundering energy of thousands of horses (Cartoon 17).

He was a great outdoorsman, not as a hunter or fisherman, but just plain outdoorsman; he could make a comfortable bed of boughs, build a tiny but efficient campfire, build a lean-to of tree limbs, or sling a canvas tarp for a shelter. He was a crack shot with rifle or pistol. He could put a pack on a horse with a diamond hitch that would hold all day, and he built his own comfortable board for backpacking. Much of this preoccupation found its way into his work.

Scott came from a distinguished family. His father was Dr. Walter Quincy Scott, an ordained Presbyterian minister, who served as president of Ohio State University and headmaster of Phillips Exeter Academy in New Hampshire. His mother was the former Cornelia Edgar of Easton, Pennsylvania, the daughter of a Presbyterian minister.

Scott's formal academic background was meager—he attended a military academy in Albany, New York, not completing the equivalent of high school—but his art training at the Art Students' League in New York City was solid. He drew political and humorous cartoons for New York City dailies for a few years, then moved to the Adirondacks with his wife and daughter, Dorothy, where he built a house and spent three more years drawing and writing. He produced a book, *The Night Riders of Cave Knob*, which won no laurels as the Great American Novel but was a tight, exciting story of violence and justice in Kentucky—illustrated, of course, by himself.

In 1912, he moved to Ellensburg, Washington, where he was secretary of the chamber of commerce, ran a delivery service, and ranched. I was born there, as was my brother Allen. Failure of the Highline Irrigation Plan to materialize drove him out of ranching, the delivery service was unsuccessful, and in 1916 he moved to Red Lodge, Montana, again as secretary of the chamber of commerce.

While there, World War I broke out. On the day war was declared, Scott attempted to enlist but was turned down; at thirty-four he was considered too old. He tried fourteen more times to enlist until he was accepted as an officer candidate in the late fall of 1918.

During this time the Scott family had moved to Missoula, Montana. Quincy Scott's first job there was selling bonds for Lincoln Life Insurance Company, but he soon realized he was competing with the Liberty Loans, which were raising money for the war effort. So when a position opened as secretary of the Missoula chamber of commerce, he accepted it.

When he entered the military service in October, 1918, he was sent to Camp Taylor, Kentucky, emerging three months later as a newly-commissioned captain. The Armistice ending World War I had been signed two months before Scott returned to Missoula in January, 1919.

In addition to his chamber work, Scott was manager of the Western Montana Fair, which featured all the thrills of the day—bronco busting, balloon ascensions, sulky racing and the like.

In 1921, the Scott family moved to Lewistown, Montana, where Quincy was once more secretary of the chamber of commerce. Before leaving Lewistown in 1924, however, he had become a full-time executive of the Boy Scouts of America.

Economic prospects in Montana were not bright. An oil boom near Lewistown petered out, and there was a succession of crop failures. The Scotts' next stop—a longer one—was Seattle. After a short tour to drum up support for the Washington State Chamber of Commerce, Quincy was hired on with Foster and Kleiser, an outdoor advertising company, where he went back to his beloved art, designing outdoor boards and lecturing on color at the University of Washington. He immersed himself in the techniques of poster work, the need for striking, splashy, sometimes austere rendering, the scope and limitations of show-card tempera as a medium, and the limitations of steel and paper outdoor board production.

He worked for Foster & Kleiser five years. In early 1930, he left the firm because he felt that his ideas and contributions in the advertising field were being appropriated by others, and he was not given the recognition he deserved. He opened a studio in the Terminal Sales Building in Seattle, and although the Great Depression was beginning to bite, he managed to survive.

In the spring of 1931, Tige Reynolds, the editorial cartoonist of the

6

Oregonian in Portland, died. Scott, who was not making a fortune as a free lance, applied for the job, and to his immense satisfaction, got it. He moved to Portland on a "look-see" basis, made a hit with the editorial powers at the *Oregonian*, and was soon named permanent cartoonist. The family moved to Portland at the end of August, 1931.

For the record, Scott's first cartoon in the *Oregonian* appeared June 1, 1931. It was titled "Hi, Fella! No Fair Playin' Hooky!" It was a plug for a school election the following day. His last cartoon appeared January 18, 1949. It was titled "Pacific Horizon," and dealt with the threat of Chinese Communism.

Scott quickly made his presence felt on the *Oregonian*. Not only was he a great draftsman — he could draw anything, and had a number of styles and techniques — but he made a tremendous effort to become known quickly in his new community. He made four or five speeches a week for a year or more, and continued a heavy speaking schedule thereafter, although in later years he charged a small honorarium for most audiences (this greatly cut down on the number of engagements).

Part of the speech, in most cases, was a "chalk talk," and part of each chalk talk were the "wigglies." Scott would ask members of the audience to make two or three lines with black chalk on newsprint, and would then turn these lines into pictures. No matter how the participants jiggled or curled the lines, Scott could always produce a recognizable object. A few times, it is true, the result would be a Dr. Seuss-like animal called a seventeen-legged biggersnoodle, or a ring-tailed ornithorhynchus, but this only enhanced Scott's reputation.

Scott's years at the *Oregonian* were not all smooth. A certified conservative, he broke early with Roosevelt's New Deal experiments. The *Oregonian* high command balked at some of his cartoons, but being basically conservative themselves, eventually approved his themes, and made it unnecessary for him to follow up his threat to resign if certain cartoons were not printed.

Another continuing problem was one of deadlines. When Scott first went to the *Oregonian*, he attended an editorial conference at 9 A.M. each morning (except Saturdays and Sundays), and then had until 3 P.M. to complete his cartoon. When he left the paper in 1949, the deadline had been moved up to 11:30 A.M. to accommodate an early afternoon first edition. This usually meant that Scott had only an hour-and-a-half to turn out a finished cartoon. His work inevitably suffered, and his later cartoons lack much of the detail and workmanship of his earlier ones. His professional pride suffered, too, because he did not want to draw that way. But there was nothing he could do about it.

Finally, in 1949, after eighteen years of seven cartoons a week, he suffered a temporary physical breakdown, and retired to Neah-kah-nie on Oregon's beautiful coast. There he lived the last fifteen years of his life with his wife, enjoying golf almost daily but doing no more drawing. He was killed in an automobile accident November 9, 1965.

Scott's work covered a great variety of subjects and appealed to the generality of *Oregonian* readers. He read widely, and conceived his own cartoon subjects. It was a rare morning when the editor asked him at the editorial conference to draw a cartoon on this or that subject. Scott would already have done his homework, and would have three or four suggestions for cartoons, one of which would inevitably touch on the subject of paramount interest that day. He would usually show his very rough thought sketches at the editorial conference, and would know, when he left the conference, exactly what he was going to draw.

He seldom used models, because his knowledge of human and animal anatomy was go great that he could draw, from memory, a person of any age and either sex. He did, however, depend heavily on the *Oregonian* library for "scrap" (for example, how does one draw the radiator of a 1922 Willys-Overland?), and he would go to the public library for material if he were really stumped. This did not happen often, however.

During most of these years, his office was on the tenth floor of the old Oregonian tower at Southwest Sixth and Alder in Portland — the paper was known as "The Old Lady of Alder Street." The 100×100-foot building rose for nine full floors, but the tenth floor was part of the much smaller tower, and Scott's work space occupied the entire floor. He had a great view of river and mountains from his north-facing window. But he had a flight of many steel-grated steps to mount and descend to and from the ninth floor, where the elevator stopped, and on busy days he was up and down those stairs, at a gallop, many times.

His favorite medium was pen, brush and ink on smooth Strathmore, but in later years the pressure of time forced him more and more to brush and crayon on toothed board. I am sure this irked him somewhat, but as noted, there was little he could do about it. He had great rapport with the "boys" in the engraving room, and they would turn handsprings to get his cartoon into metal if he had trouble with his deadline.

He was a full member of the community. He was state commander of the American Legion in Montana, president of the City Club of Portland, president of the Portland chapter of the Reserve Officers Association, chairman of the Portland Chamber's Military Affairs Committee, and an elder of the Presbyterian Church.

It was largely due to his efforts that Willamette National Cemetery was established in Portland. He was active in Republican politics, spoke at many political rallies and conventions, and in 1938 was urged to run for governor of Oregon — a possibility he discarded when Charles Sprague, publisher of the *Oregon Statesman* in Salem, entered the lists.

The only interruption in his tenure as cartoonist came during World

War II. Some months before Pearl Harbor he went on active duty as a lieutenant colonel, was assigned to the Morale Division in Washington, D.C., and was there until he reached the mandatory separation age of sixty in September, 1942.

Also, in later years, his workload was reduced to six cartoons a week, with Ralph Lee filling in on the seventh day, as well as during Scott's annual vacations.

Scott's aim as a cartoonist was not to make people laugh—although he often did—but to inform them, through a telling picture, exactly what the "guts" of a complex situation were. He often said, "Almost anybody can draw a funny picture, but does it really tell the truth about the situation?"

To him, truth and honor were more than words. They were a way of life. And so long as he could live that life in the West he loved, he was a happy man.

THE BEST
OF
QUINCY SCOTT

1 *Quincy Scott*

Plenty O' Small Game, Too!
28 June 1931

"Scarface Al" Capone got his nickname from a razor slash on his left cheek, ear to lip, received in a brawl when he was a young man. When Johnny Torrio left Chicago, Capone became the undisputed leader of the mob there, and in 1927 his wealth was estimated at $100 million.

He remained immune from prosecution for many crimes, including the St. Valentine's Day murder, when his henchmen killed eight rival gang members. But, in June, 1931, he was indicted for income tax evasion. Found guilty in October, Capone was sentenced to eleven years in prison, plus a $70,000 fine.

Headlines in newspapers on June 27 read, "Sixty-one Capone aides in Federal net; new indictment affects outside provinces; total under charges 129." The charges involved failure to pay income tax on the sale of more than four million gallons of alcohol in four states (which did not include Illinois, presumably because the sales had to be in interstate commerce).

Capone served time in Atlanta and Alcatraz, and was released in 1939, a slack-jawed paretic.

2 Quincy Scott

Wrong Remedies Right No Wrongs
3 August 1931

Economic tensions ran high during the depression, and low prices for raw milk resulted in a strike by producing dairymen against distributors in the Portland area in the summer of 1931. Headlines read, "Dairymen Fight to Hold Up Milk," "Portland in State of Siege," "Soldiers Guard Roads," "Conflict Between City and Country."

Many farmers, rather than deliver milk to the distributors or run the gauntlet of striking dairymen, dumped their milk into streams. Milk is one crop that has to be harvested, because of the biological nature of the cow, and dumping was the only alternative to delivery.

Fortunately, the strike was short, and was ended by Julius Meier, governor of Oregon, in an arrangement between the warring parties, which saw the price settled at $2.175 per hundredweight—a price that presumably satisfied neither the dairymen nor the producers, but that they were willing to live with in lieu of no income at all.

This type of action was common during the 1930s, and preceded the famous killing of the young pigs only a couple of years later.

3 *Quincy Scott*

Let 'Er Buck!
28 August 1931

One does not have to be an Oregonian to appreciate the excitement and thrills of a top-notch rodeo, and the Pendleton Round-Up has ranked among the best western shows for many years.

Drawing a tough cowhand aboard a mean bronco was pure delight for Quincy Scott, and this cartoon is included because it catches the rodeo spirit as well as an artist could.

The Indians in the picture are no accident, as they have been part of the scene at the Round-Up since its inception.

16

4 *Quincy Scott*

Uncle Is About Sold on the Project
20 September 1931

It comes as a surprise to many people that the idea of the Columbia Basin irrigation project, involving Grand Coulee Dam and the large-scale works that accompanied it, antedated the New Deal.

As a matter of fact, Rufus Woods, publisher of the *Wenatchee World*, had been preaching the irrigation of the Columbia Basin for many years before this cartoon appeared. And the planning of the Irrigation League and other bodies was pretty well along before President Roosevelt and Congress told the Bureau of Reclamation to go ahead with Grand Coulee.

Quincy Scott's interest in irrigation dated back at least as far as 1912, when, as secretary of the Ellensburg (Washington) Chamber of Commerce, he helped promote the Highline Project in Kittitas County, which did not come to fruition at that time.

18

5 *Quincy Scott*

Peace Dove: "I Suppose You'll Tell Me It's Not on Your Beat!"
23 September 1931

On September 18, 1931, the Japanese army in Kwangtung, claiming that an explosion on the Japanese-owned Manchuria Railroad had been caused by Chinese saboteurs, seized the arsenals of Mukden and several neighboring cities.

The twin policemen of peace, the Kellogg Pact and the League of Nations, look on with studied indifference as Japan goes after Manchuria. The "peacekeeping machinery" set up after World War I thus failed its first severe test, as it was to fail later when Italy invaded Ethiopia and Japan invaded China.

The Manchurian "incident" was significant mainly in marking the end of any pretense of international peacekeeping, and the beginning of a long series of aggressions ending with World War II.

6 *Quincy Scott*

A Most Gallant Trophy, Sir Thomas
4 October 1931

Thomas Lipton, who owned tea plantations in Ceylon and a hogpacking house in Chicago, was known as "the world's best loser," because of his expensive hobby—challenging the New York Yacht Club for the America's Cup, a relatively inexpensive piece of hardware that has become the most famous trophy in international yacht racing.

Lipton made five unsuccessful challenges for the trophy between 1899 and 1930, his yacht bearing the names *Shamrock I* through *V.*

Born in 1850 in Glasgow, Scotland, Lipton came to the United States in 1865 and worked at manual occupations for many years, returning to Glasgow in 1876. There he opened a small grocery store that he developed into the largest commercial establishment in the United Kingdom. It was from this start that he branched into the plantation and packing businesses. He was knighted in 1898, and died October 2, 1931.

7 *Quincy Scott*

But It Did
2 November 1931

Noah must have felt about the deluge the same way most Americans felt about the economy in the early years of the depression—"It ain't never goin' to clear up!" Noah and the Americans had something else in common: Even if they hoped in their heart of hearts that it *would* clear up, they had no idea *when*.

Quincy Scott knew it would clear up someday. But, while expressing optimism, even he could not predict the date by which the economic storm would be over. Elsewhere in this volume are cartoons and comments on the same subject. Scott drew many. After all, it was the overriding theme of the times: "When is this blankety-blank depression going to be over?" Politicians made promises, but not even the wisest economists had the answers.

Quincy Scott

He Sticks His Head in the Lion's Mouth
—and Greets You with a Smile!
5 January 1932

It is remarkable that in a subcontinent of more than 300 million souls, one man should be so dominant on the social and political scene that his name would become synonymous with the Indian freedom movement.

Mohandas K. Gandhi was that man. (His more familiar title, "Mahatma," is reserved in India for persons of great spiritual eminence.)

As a lawyer, Gandhi fought for the civil rights of Indians in South Africa for some twenty years, with considerable success. His principles of civil disobedience and non-cooperation with civil authority were practiced there.

In 1914 he returned to India, and immediately became a leader in the struggle for home rule. This Scott cartoon came during one of the many episodes when Gandhi declared a new campaign of civil disobedience and non-cooperation. Despite his many arrests, fasts and releases from prison, his campaigns were largely responsible for Britain granting India's independence in 1947.

9 *Quincy Scott*

A Ride in a Rickshaw
30 March 1932

Japan followed up its initial seizure of Chinese arsenals in Manchuria five months earlier by forcing withdrawal of Chinese troops from the entire area, entirely without official sanction of the Japanese government. Manchuria was then established as an independent state, Manchukuo, controlled by Japan through the puppet Henry Pu-Yi. All pretense of party government in Japan was abandoned as a result of the occupation of Manchuria, and control of Japanese affairs slipped into the hands of a powerful military clique.

Although the League of Nations did not take formal action against Japan for another two years, Japan's conquest of Manchuria drew the censure of nations throughout the free world, and as Scott noted, "Japan left the fellowship of enlightened nations."

28

10 *Quincy Scott*

Is This a Forgotten Man?
7 July 1932

Quincy Scott traced his beginnings as a cartoonist to turn-of-the-century New York, and this figure representing corrupt saloon politics was right out of that period. It was, in a way, an anachronism, because the saloon by that name did not return to America after the repeal of prohibition, largely because most states followed up repeal with very restrictive state laws, such as Oregon's Knox Act.

When this cartoon was drawn, however, repeal was still only a plank in the Democratic platform, and Scott had no way of knowing that state legislators would turn out to be almost as wary of "saloon politics" as he.

11 Quincy Scott

H'm–m–m– You Can Begin to Sit up a Little—but Go Easy!
6 August 1932

Like the famous "light at the end of the tunnel" during the Vietnam War, "prosperity is just around the corner" was a recurring theme in American journalism from the moment of the stock market crash in October, 1929. No one in public life correctly predicted the length or depth of the Great Depression.

The subject of this cartoon, however, was better timed than most, since the summer of 1932 marked the actual low point in the stock market averages. From that point on the market recovered slowly, in a long series of fits and starts—in much the same manner in which it had descended to that low point during the preceding three years.

32

12 *Quincy Scott*

Sweeping Back the Ocean with a Broom
18 September 1932

The presidential election campaign of 1932 was just warming up when this cartoon appeared, and Quincy Scott was skeptical of Franklin Roosevelt's ability to bring about recovery and end unemployment while maintaining a balanced budget. The election proved that the public was more interested in recovery and employment than it was in deficits and surpluses.

It might be recalled that Keynesian theories were neither preached nor accepted by either major political party in 1932, and Roosevelt's professed economics were just as conservative as those of his opponent, Herbert Hoover. When push came to shove, however, theory went out the window, and the Democrats ran the deficits they felt they needed to get the country moving again.

34

13 *Quincy Scott*

'Ere Y'are, Sam'l—H'and I Feel Better Orlready!
17 December 1932

Much was made of the fact that England continued to make payments to the United States on its World War I debts even during the depression, but as a matter of grim fact the payments were more symbolic than substantial. England was the heaviest Allied borrower from the U.S. during World War I, receiving a total of nearly five billion dollars, about a billion more than France, the second-leading borrower. Italy was third with two billion, and no other nation borrowed as much as a billion.

Britain made payments of only four-and-one-third million dollars on principal, but did pay more than a billion-and-a-half in interest. However, principal and interest due and unpaid had amounted to nearly nine billion by 1972, according to the Treasury Department.

Finland received much credit for paying all its World War I debt to the U.S., amounting to only nine million dollars, but fewer know that Cuba, Lithuania and Nicaragua also removed their debts; Cuba's being the largest in this group—ten million.

(Armenia borrowed nearly twelve million from the U.S. during World War I and to date has repaid $17.49!)

14 QUINCY Scott

Gimme!
15 June 1933

Hands stretched across the sea for American dollars have become a common phenomenon in recent years, but it really dates no farther back than the depression, when countries whose currencies were weaker than ours saw the dollar as a refuge from economic ills.

Ironically, the U.S.A. did not operate a foreign-aid program during the 1930s because we had obligations at home that caused the federal government to run what seemed at the time to be horrendous deficits.

The nearest we came to overseas handouts was a moratorium on World War I war debts, and this eventually metamorphosed into cancelation in all but a handful of cases.

15 *Quincy Scott*

But Tough on the Man on the Flying Trapeze
26 June 1933

That pitiable character, variously known as U.S. Taxpayer and John Q. Public, shows little stomach for the job assigned him here — catching and supporting the vast bulk of World War I debts upon which the nations involved were defaulting during the depression.

American investors had earlier lost a few billions in the widespread defaulting on government and private securities issued after World War I. There were Brazilian railroad bonds, Peruvian hydroelectric bonds, and other securities bearing fancy interest rates — securities that went "poof" at the first sign of depression. Some token payoffs have been made in the long years since the early 1930s, but in general the worldwide structure of debt that was built up prior to the depression was simply written off.

"She floats through the air with the greatest of ease"

16 *Quincy Scott*

Giving Us the Go-by
13 July 1933

It is difficult to realize that many Americans, including Quincy Scott, were fighting the environmental battle as early as 1933, when the nation faced so many other pressing matters. But there was no dodging the fact that the Willamette, polluted by domestic and industrial wastes from dozens of communities along its banks, was not fit for fishing, boating or swimming in that year.

Oregon was among the first states to start attacking pollution. And abetted by federal legislation and dollars, the Willamette again supports a fair salmon fishery and is a favorite haunt for boaters. At most times of year, it is also safe for swimming.

The clean-up fight was a long and costly one, involving principally the installation of expensive equipment by many types of industries to keep pollutants out of the river and installation by cities of secondary treatment plants to insure a cleaner effluent from sewage-treatment facilities.

17 *Quincy Scott*

Capture
14 July 1933

This is the definitive cartoon on the harnessing of the Columbia River's horsepower by the first in a rather daring system of dams.

Roosevelt's plan for a lower river dam referred, of course, to Bonneville. Although the date indicates that the plan was introduced early in Roosevelt's first administration, it was quickly authorized as a Public Works Administration project and work soon began.

The engineering for the dam was so hasty, in fact, that the first cofferdam for the spillway at the upper (east) end of Bradford Island was washed out during high water, and the site for the dam was actually moved a few hundred yards downstream.

One had to see the Columbia River during its June flood, when it was swollen by melting snow and rain to flows as high as 1,200,000 cubic feet per second to realize the problems faced by the dam builders. But the problems were overcome, and the dam was dedicated by President Roosevelt in 1937.

18 *Quincy Scott*

The End of the Trail
7 November 1933

Patterned after the famous painting of the same title, featuring an Indian with head bowed mounted on a drooping horse, this cartoon is a monument to the end of the always controversial Eighteenth Amendment, which, with the enabling Volstead Act, brought prohibition to the United States in 1919.

The election in November 1933 signaled the repeal of prohibition, although it was another month before the Utah legislature, as the 36th state body, ratified the repealing amendment.

The Eighteenth Amendment forbade "the manufacture, sale, transportation within, importation to or exportation from" the United States of any alcoholic beverage (defined by law as that containing more than one-half of one percent alcohol). Home brew, bathtub gin, home-fermented wine and "mountain dew" or "Kentucky lightning" were all banned under the manufacturing provision, although this aspect of prohibition was widely disregarded during its fourteen years of existence.

Since repeal, some states have permitted the making of small amounts of beer and wine at home, although distillation and sale of hard liquor is forbidden everywhere except upon payment of federal and state taxes. Indeed, the loss of revenue to the federal government from taxes on alcohol for consumption, estimated today at five hundred million dollars annually, was one of the principal arguments for repeal.

46

19 *QUINCY SCOTT*

Of Course There'll be Mistletoe at the House-Party
26 December 1933

This cartoon was early recognition of the phenomenon that would later be known as the "coalition" between conservative southern Democrats and the Republicans. Never a formal organization, the coalition's strength varied from time to time depending on the particular issues involved. There is no question that it was operational from early in the New Deal until recent years.

President Roosevelt wielded enough power to keep the coalition from being very effective, but it acted as a brake on many New Deal programs.

QUINCY Scott

Descent from Mount Jefferson
17 January 1934

Of the over six thousand cartoons drawn by Quincy Scott during his eighteen years on the *Oregonian*, this one certainly stands among the three or four most important.

It was drawn at the time of the passage of the Gold Reserve Act, which empowered the president to fix the weight of the dollar at not more than sixty percent nor less than fifty percent of its then existing weight (23.22 grains of pure gold). The effect of the act, of course, was the devaluation of the dollar by nearly half, and Scott regarded this as a breach of faith by the government, for the American people had engaged in millions of contracts, mortgages, purchases and sales with the prior value of the dollar as the measure of value.

After Scott had drawn this cartoon, he showed it to other members of the editorial staff, and the editor showed it to the publisher. Neither of the latter two wanted it printed, since they felt the newspaper should support the New Deal in this action, although the newspaper normally opposed Roosevelt and the New Deal. Scott, however, said he would resign if the cartoon were not run, and after heated controversy the decision was made to print it.

For those not familiar with Oregon geography, there is indeed a Mount Jefferson, second highest peak in the state, although Scott was here quoting President Thomas Jefferson and the importance of keeping the faith of the people.

21 *Quincy Scott*

A Test of the Steersman's Ability
22 January 1934

Problems of school finance in Oregon were not new in 1934, and they have continued to this day.

Periodically, a general sales tax has been put forward as the soundest method of providing a greater measure of state support for the public schools, but it has never gotten past the electorate. Sales tax measures passed by the legislature have invariably gone down to defeat in referenda, and it has almost become an article of faith in Oregon politics that support of a sales tax is the kiss-of-death to political aspirations.

During the depression property taxes were in many cases confiscatory, since people without jobs simply could not pay them. Many sheriff's sales were held throughout the state for non-payment of taxes, and a number of fortunes were founded by people who had funds to pick up the foreclosed properties for a few cents on the dollar.

This was one of the factors that placed the schools in such a desperate position during the depression—and why teachers' salaries in some of the poorer districts (when they were paid at all) hovered around five hundred dollars per year.

Better Mend the Bridge Than Fly Old Dobbin
24 October 1934

Quincy Scott was one of those peculiar throwbacks to whom confidence in the national currency was a primary article of faith. He viewed the lack of such confidence on the part of businessmen as a primary reason for prolonging the depression at a time when business should have been on the rebound.

Appearing as it did about two weeks before the 1934 mid-term election, it is likely that Scott was trying to influence voters to return Republicans to the House and Senate. Efforts like his were largely unsuccessful, however, as the Republicans lost strength in both houses.

His thesis was accurate, however, as business confidence in the administration was very slow to pick up, largely as a result of Roosevelt's fiscal and monetary policies.

Quincy Scott

Another Major Kidnaping
15 November 1934

America has known many political bosses, but there is probably no other instance in which a politician so thoroughly dominated the affairs of an entire state as Huey Pierce Long did in Louisiana in the mid-1930s.

Defeated for the office of governor in 1924, he ran successfully in 1928 and immediately set about installing his friends in important political posts. He was impeached in 1929 on charges of bribery and misappropriation of state funds; the case was later dropped, however, and he was cleared of the charges.

In 1930 he was elected to the U.S. Senate. At first a supporter of Roosevelt's New Deal, he soon thereafter began to fight openly against its various reforms. He put forward a popular Share-the-Wealth program, which would have guaranteed $5,000 a year to every family. While this was never adopted, it marked him as an unalterable Populist.

By 1935 he was virtual dictator of Louisiana, but he did not enjoy his power long as he was assassinated in September of that year.

24 *Quincy Scott*

A Suggestion from the Mayor
16 December 1934

Portland's mayor was Joe Carson. And he was in favor of tearing up the tracks for streetcars in Portland and replacing them with trolley buses.

This was done, in fact, and the rubber-tired trolley buses, with their twin-overhead trolleys, were familiar sights on Portland streets until the 1950s, when the transit company turned to a gasoline and diesel fleet.

Today (1980) the mass transit people are talking about "light rail," and it would be ironic indeed to see tracks laid again from the suburbs to the downtown area.

As Quincy Scott was fond of saying, "The one thing we learn from history is that we learn nothing from history."

58

25

"For This Relief, Much Thanks" — Hamlet
21 January 1935

This cartoon epitomizes the situation that has existed since the start of the New Deal—Uncle Sam preempting (with individual and corporate income taxes) much of the states' taxing authority, and the states (along with the counties and cities) looking in turn to Uncle Sam for various forms of subsidy.

Federal revenue-sharing did not come into existence until long after Quincy Scott left the *Oregonian*, but if he had still been doing cartoons when revenue-sharing came to pass, he could have resurrected this one and run it again.

The human frailty evident here is captured in the phrase, "Robbing Peter to pay Paul." We all know perfectly well what is happening, but we all think that if we can only get federal funding for a pet project, all our problems will be solved.

26 *Quincy Scott*

Canine Spring Style Opening
19 March 1935

This is another "watershed" cartoon. Behind it lay the Versailles Treaty of 1919; ahead of it lay World War II. The rearmed dachshund personifies Hitler's breach of the Versailles Treaty; the rearmament of Germany for the first time after World War I.

Students of history generally agree that if the Allies of the earlier war had called Hitler's bluff and sent troops back into Germany, he would have reassessed his plans to dominate the world. But he guessed correctly that the Allies would not act—and so on to *Anschluss* with Austria, the Munich Pact, Czechoslovakia—and Poland.

27 *Quincy Scott*

Mechanical Rabbit
10 May 1935

No matter how fast the greyhound runs, he never catches up with the mechanical rabbit, and no matter how fast "We, the People," run, we are never going to catch up with inflation. This may have seemed a rather abusrd proposition in 1935, when the nation was just creeping out of the depression and prices were still low, but the process had already set in, and has never been halted for very long since.

Perhaps the analogy is not exact, since the speed of the rabbit is matched to the speed of the greyhound, while the rate of inflation sometimes exceeds the ability of the people to keep prices in view. But with greyhound racing fairly new in Oregon, Quincy Scott found the similarities close enough to inspire this amusing cartoon.

28 *Quincy Scott*

No

26 May 1935

Many forget that Portland, generally considered a staid, conservative town, was caught up in the wave of gangsterism that swept the United States during and after prohibition. Among other activities, Portland saw the vandalizing of dry-cleaning plants that would not obtain "protection," and there was talk that various organized mobs were trying to move into the city.

This phenomenon, akin to the scattering of rats that accompanies the destruction of an old warehouse, is fairly common in America. When gangs saturate an area or become subject to legal action, they look for new "turf," a place less hostile to their activities, or less able to protect itself. Additionally, gangs are always looking for new sources of revenue, and any "soft touches" in virgin territory are eagerly sought.

But official corruption, always necessary to the free flowering gangs, has never reached significant heights in Portland.

29 *Quincy Scott*

What! No Wheels?
1 June 1935

The National Recovery Administration (NRA) was a keystone in the New Deal recovery structure. It was the administrative body created to carry out the provisions of the National Industrial Recovery Act, which sought to promote a strengthened economy through reduction in working hours, establishment of minimum wages and mitigation of price-cutting caused by intense competition. This was accomplished through the promulgation of industrial codes, which covered approximately ninety-eight percent of American industry within eighteen months of the act's adoption in 1933.

Under its familiar seal of the blue eagle, the NRA enjoyed some success in stimulating industrial growth, with a fair degree of cooperation from industry. But in May, 1935, the U.S. Supreme Court declared the act unconstitutional, on the grounds that Congress could not delegate legislative authority to such an agency, and that the codes illegally applied to intrastate commerce.

The effect of the decision was to take the steam out of many of the agencies that had sprung up under the New Deal, although in all truth the NRA had already accomplished much of what President Roosevelt had hoped it would do.

30 *Quincy Scott*

Worry at the Three-Quarter Post
6 September 1935

Appearing one year before the fall campaign of 1936, this cartoon illustrated the concern of citizens who shared Quincy Scott's political views that, if Roosevelt were to be renominated and reelected, the good credit of the nation might continue to be given second place in the making of national policy, with the "tax-tax, spend-spend, elect-elect" group remaining in authority.

The departure from the gold standard and the continued decline in the value of the dollar were already realities at this early date. But the public liked the heady brew of the many forms of federal subsidies they were getting, and it is history, of course, that FDR continued from the three-quarter post to win by a landslide over Alf Landon at the finish.

31 *Quincy Scott*

Lesson in Un-na-tur-al His-to-ry
16 October 1935

So far as the author knows, Quincy Scott was the first to translate "New Deal" into "Gnu Deal," and to use the gnu rather than the Democratic donkey in many cartoons symbolizing activities of the administration. He supported his analogy by the list of attributes, noted in the cartoon, that indeed make the gnu out to be a "funny animal."

Those who did not live through those trying times would have a hard time understanding the ferment abroad in the land—the multitude of ideas put forward by the "Brain Trusters," the Townsend Plan, Technocracy as advocated by Howard Scott and others, the EPIC (End Poverty in California) plan, the flood of edicts and programs from the "alphabet soup" agencies in Washington, the antics of an ever-present lunatic fringe, to say nothing of the thunder from the right—Dr. Gerald L.K. Smith, the Ku Klux Klan and others.

Habitat: The Cities of America
22 November 1935

Gangsters and hoodlums were much in the news in the United States during the Great Depression. The submachine gun, carried in a violin case by a sinister figure wearing dark glasses, a broad-rimmed fedora, a dark shirt and white tie, was the popular cliché for the gangland figure. Phrases such as "wearing concrete overshoes" and "being taken for a ride" became part of the general vocabulary.

Why gangsterism became so prominent during this period can be debated. It may be explained by the fact that the mobs were trying to carve out new territories following the repeal of prohibition and loss of revenue, plus the fact that the depression itself, with its unemployment, left few alternatives for some of the gang members.

33 **Birth Pangs**
29 January 1936

A Quincy Scott self-portrait: trying to give birth to a new cartoon, while his ears are assailed by the traffic noises from Sixth Avenue, Broadway, Alder and Washington streets. His office was on the tenth floor of the Oregonian tower, which meant it caught noise from all four sides—auto horns, streetcar bells, trucks thundering, perhaps gears clashing as inexperienced drivers took off at intersections.

Although given a cartoonist's slight exaggeration, this cartoon is a pretty accurate depiction of "Q.S." from the rear. It is included in this anthology partly for its humor, and partly to give the reader a better understanding of the conditions under which Scott worked.

34 *Quincy Scott*

Curtain
4 April 1936

A grim cartoon on a grim subject—the electrocution of Bruno Hauptmann, a carpenter, for the kidnap-murder of Charles Augustus Lindbergh, Jr., from his home in Hopewell, New Jersey on March 1, 1932
(The Lindbergh baby was twenty months old at the time).

Many thought the crime would never be solved, and there were many
false leads, but authorities got a break when Hauptmann passed one of
the ransom bills, and $14,000 more in marked money was found in his
garage. Other evidence, including a ladder, linked Hauptmann to the
crime.

Largely because of the trauma from and publicity linked to these
events, the Lindberghs moved their permanent home to England. Later,
during World War II, Lindbergh performed yeoman civilian service for
the United States.

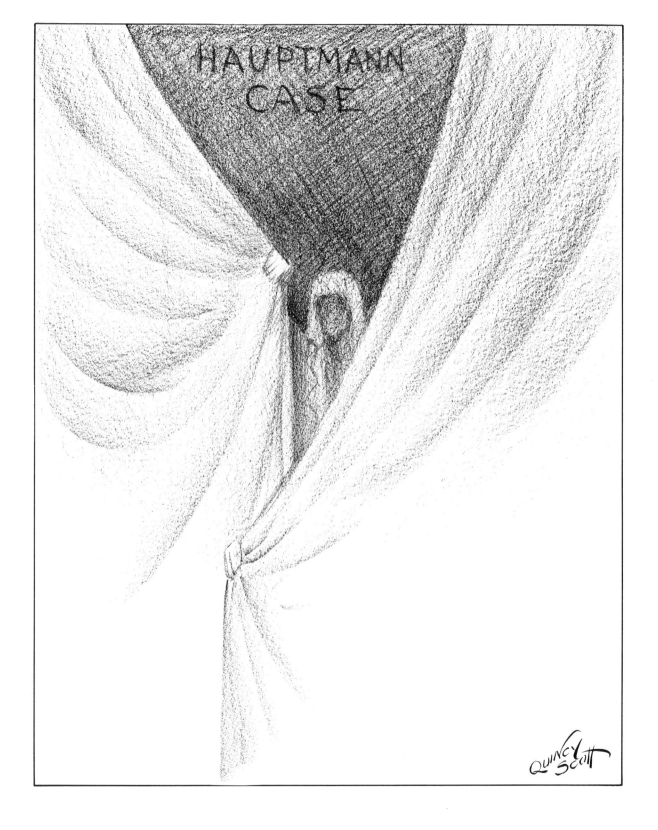

35 *Quincy Scott*

East Side, West Side
22 July 1936

Alfred Emanuel Smith, four-term governor of New York and Democratic candidate for president in 1928, is shown in this cartoon doing a fast waltz with the zoological emblem of the Republican party. The cartoon won for Scott an honorable mention in the Pulitzer Prize competition.

Smith was soundly defeated by Herbert Hoover in the 1928 presidential election, and although he remained titular head of the Democratic party, he was beaten by his fellow New Yorker and Democratic governor, Franklin D. Roosevelt, in the convention of 1932. Roosevelt went on to win the presidency against Hoover, and his success did not endear him to Smith.

While Smith turned to various business enterprises, including a prominent position in the consortium that built the Empire State Building, he was never on friendly terms with Roosevelt. Smith was a social liberal, but he was an economic conservative, and Roosevelt's New Deal did not sit well with him.

If there was any surprise in Smith's public support of the Republicans in 1936, when this cartoon appeared, it was that he went public, and did not keep his thoughts to himself.

The caption of the cartoon, consisting of the first four words of "The Sidewalks of New York," is extremely apt, since it not only epitomizes Al Smith's big-city background but also enables the reader to hum a few bars as he pictures him dancing with the GOP elephant.

80

36 Quincy Scott

The Golden Egg That Laid out the Goose
26 July 1936

The cost of the New Deal was appalling to Quincy Scott, as to many
other people. Some feel that the cost is firmly built into the structure of
our current national debt. The 1936 dollars that Quincy Scott was talking
about would seem like chickenfeed today.

37 *Quincy Scott*

Spirit of '36?
26 August 1936

Here is Quincy Scott's trenchant commentary on what he felt to be the basic weakness of the welfare state: given an option between a free ride and earning one's way, a disturbing number would opt for the free ride.

Hitchhiking did not really become a national phenomenon until the 1930s. Before that, if a driver saw a man with his thumb out beside the road, the assumption was that the man had had car trouble or had run out of gas.

But the depression did not stifle the burning desire of Americans to move around, to see if the grass was greener on the other side of the fence. If anything, it stimulated this desire. And with jobs and money at a premium, the number of people seeking a free ride to almost anyplace increased manyfold.

Scott saw hitchhiking as simply another "something for nothing" symptom among the many that beset the country in those trying years.

Quincy Scott

Quincy Scott

Shades of Simon Legree: "I Was Small Time!"
28 October 1936

"No vote, no relief. No vote, no job." That, as Quincy Scott viewed it, was the legend Jim Farley carried on his whip as chairman of the national Democratic Central Committee.

There is no question that Roosevelt used his political power to the utmost in controlling appointments available to the party chiefs, and there is also no question that those appointed at the lower echelons favored Democrats when it came to handing out patronage plums.

The extent to which political considerations controlled who received Work Projects Administration jobs could be debated, but after years of unemployment thousands swallowed their political convictions in favor of a meal ticket. And the New Dealers were past-masters at the art of funneling government job funds into areas where important elections might be in doubt.

Scott viewed the New Deal as a giant political machine in the Tammany tradition, and this cartoon, like several others, was a graphic expression of this belief.

39 *Quincy Scott*

David Windsor Chooses
11 December 1936

There is very little that words can add to the impact of this cartoon. It was recognition of the fact that King Edward VIII had turned his back on the crown to marry the American Wallis Simpson, "The woman I love," precipitating a major crisis in England.

40 *Quincy Scott*

So That's Me!
30 April 1937

Quincy Scott must have had a lot of fun drawing this cartoon. The slick, clean-shaven young pioneer standing atop Oregon's new capitol building, with his tight pants and tight shirt—and covered with gold leaf in the bargain—must have seemed an anomalous figure to those familiar with the real pioneers.

So much time has passed since the capitol building was opened in 1938 that Oregonians scarcely glance at the figure any more, unless they happen to be approaching Salem from the south and catch the sun glancing off the gold leaf of the statue.

SHADE OF
OREGON
PIONEER

STATUE FOR
TOP OF NEW
STATE HOUSE

QUINCY SCOTT

41 *Quincy Scott*

Consent of the Governed?
14 May 1937

Roosevelt's attempt to pack the Supreme Court by increasing its number from nine to fifteen members was the issue of the day when this cartoon appeared.

Scott's vigorous protest was in the minds of many, Democrats and Republicans alike. Congressmen who supported Roosevelt on most if not all other issues deserted him on this one, for if the president had his way on this issue, it would be virtually impossible to refuse him on any others, since an enlarged Supreme Court could be expected to support the president's viewpoint.

Both Roosevelt and his detractors may not have considered fully the historical fact that persons appointed to the Supreme Court often shed political positions, and become more independent and objective. Thus it is possible that even if Roosevelt had packed the court with hand-picked "liberals," he may have found them as intractable as the old court.

QUINCY Scott

"A Plague on Both Your Houses!"
15 July 1937

It is no coincidence that this cartoon followed the previous one by just one day. But it expresses a very different viewpoint. The issue of the packed court was certainly one of the three or four most crucial during Roosevelt's four terms (along with gold devaluation, the welfare progam and lend-lease). Roosevelt stirred up a hornet's nest with his court-packing proposal.

When he tried to initiate a constitutional amendment by getting a resolution to this effect through Congress, both houses said, "No." This action by Congress marked a watershed in Roosevelt's tenure. Until this time, he had had his way on all critical issues, but the court-packing defeat proved he could be beaten.

43 *Quincy Scott*

Board or Club?
29 July 1937

The question raised by this cartoon was whether the newly created National Labor Relations Board (NLRB) was to be a truly independent body, acting as an impartial arbiter and enforcer of labor law, or a tool of labor, personified here by John L. Lewis, the moving force behind the Congress of Industrial Organizations (CIO). There was a real fear that the board, if too compliant to the wishes of labor leaders, would further strengthen labor and weaken business.

History has shown that this fear was largely unjustified, and that, especially since 1947 with the passage of the Taft-Hartley Act, labor has had as much reason to complain about the board as has business. The fact that the NLRB has not been in the news in recent years is testimony that it is performing its principal function — calling and overseeing elections to determine which union, if any, is going to represent employees in a particular company or industry.

QUINCY SCOTT

44 *Quincy Scott*

"Home Is the Sailor, Home from the Sea"
7 February 1938

In Robert Louis Stevenson's "Requiem" one finds the lines, "Home is the sailor, home from the sea, and the hunter home from the hill." Quincy Scott borrowed from this poem in describing the 1938 homecoming of the battleship *Oregon*. The *Oregon* first came to public prominence during the Spanish-American War when, in 1898, it made a historic 15,000-mile, 47-day dash, under full steam, from the Pacific coast to Cuba (to the great surprise of the Spanish high command). This trip had to be made around Cape Horn, because it antedated the Panama Canal, and was cited as one of the reasons the canal had to be built.

During World War II, when the demand for steel became critical, most of the superstructure of the *Oregon* was scrapped, but its mast was left to the city of Portland, and today forms the focal point of Portland Park Waterfront along the Willamette River.

45 *Quincy Scott*

Uncle Knows
23 June 1938

Although he was a teetotaler himself (until after World War II, when he would take a highball in the late afternoon), Quincy Scott was worldly enough to recognize the causes of a hangover. He saw the close analogy between Uncle Sam's carefree borrowing policies and the classic line of the barfly, "One more isn't going to hurt me."

This cartoon was drawn when the United States was heading into the recession of 1938, and the federal government was prescribing Roosevelt's favorite "lend-spend" nostrum. It is commonly asserted, and probably true, that the depression did not really end until World War II, and there is no way of knowing whether or when the hangover predicted by Scott would have come to pass without the war.

46

Quincy Scott

Splitting Hairs
28 June 1938

Quincy Scott really enjoyed sticking the needle into FDR when the president was guilty of contradictory, self-serving statements, as was clearly the case in this instance. Before the 1938 mid-term elections, Roosevelt piously stated that he would not interfere with the state and local choices of candidates in the primaries, but on another occasion said that as national head of the Democratic party, he would certainly make his wishes known.

This type of ambivalence is common in politics — in fact, it is part of the warp and woof of practical politics — but cartoonists of all wavelengths of the political spectrum delight in making an issue of it.

The use of the axe as an instrument of hair-splitting is probably not accidental; Scott was probably saying that if any local party sachems objected, the axe would keep on going and split the skull as well as the hair.

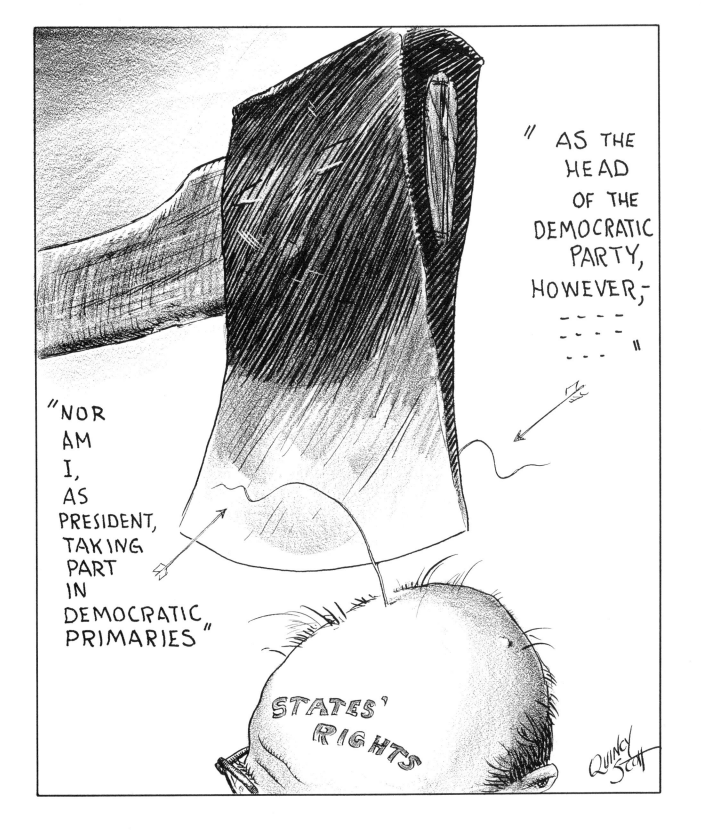

47

QUINCY Scott

If History Repeats, Where Now is Wellington?
23 September 1938

This cartoon coincides with the Munich conference in which the World
War I Allies, Britain and France, agreed to the occupation of the
Sudetenland in Czechoslovakia by the Germans. If one does not include
the annexation of Austria by Germany in March, 1938, the occupation of
the Sudetenland marked the first "conquest" of foreign territory by Hitler,
and doubtless inspired Scott to compare Hitler with the French emperor
of the early nineteenth century.

The cartoon comparison, of course, is not flattering to Hitler. It is obvious that Scott did not consider him the equal of Napoleon. It is equally
obvious that Scott accurately foresaw that Hitler's appetite would not be
satisfied with a piece of Czechoslovakia. What Scott sensed, but which
could not be predicted at that date (unless one believed all the words of
Mein Kampf) was that Hitler had embarked on a program of world
conquest.

The question, "Where now is Wellington?", was a very good one. No
one had an answer in September, 1938. The historical answer, of course,
is that there were many Wellingtons—Churchill, Roosevelt, Stalin, their
top field commanders, even de Gaulle. What matters is that these Wellingtons *did* come forth.

48 *Quincy Scott*

Israel in the Land of Captivity
25 November 1938

The plight of the Jew in Nazi Germany is pithily described in this cartoon. Hitler would not permit Jews to emigrate—but he made conditions insupportable for them at home, boycotting their businesses, keeping their sons and daughters out of universities, denying them government jobs. Police turned their backs on Nazi hoodlums burning Jewish stores, and the Gestapo made things very tough for Jews trying to slip through the border, although thousands did.

Hitler's "final solution" of the gas chambers at Dachau, Buchenwald and other concentration camps was not yet at hand, but it was not far off.

The Biblical reference to the captivities in Egypt and Babylon is clear, but it is doubtful that the Jewish people suffered more in those times than it did in Germany between 1933 and 1945.

49

A Bit Too Much
7 February 1939

The date on this cartoon is immaterial; it could have appeared at any time from the beginning of the New Deal to the present. The image of the little fellow in business bogged down in a sea of regulations and paperwork required by the federal government is universally recognized.

It is interesting, however, that Scott managed to use a horse in his characterization. His use of a pun in the title, "A bit too much," justifies this decision, although Scott never needed an excuse to draw a horse.

50 *Quincy Scott*

Can't say "Nine Old Men" Now
17 April 1939

Justice William O. Douglas was only forty years old when he was appointed to the Supreme Court by President Roosevelt in the spring of 1939. The thought of Douglas sprinting up the steps of the Supreme Court Building is hard to reconcile with images of the man in his old age, but he was always an outdoorsman and could easily have entered the court building in just that way.

The reference to "nine old men" relates to Roosevelt's characterization of the Supreme Court at the time he was trying to get Congress to initiate an amendment to the Constitution increasing the number of justices from nine to fifteen.

Some of the most famous liberal members of the court, such as Brandeis and Holmes, served until they were quite old, but Roosevelt did not let this fact stand in the way of his debatable argument that old age equates with conservatism.

51

Hooking on
18 June 1939

The formation of what was to become the Northwest Power Grid had its beginning and backbone in a transmission line connecting Bonneville Dam on the lower Columbia River with Grand Coulee Dam east of Wenatchee, Washington. The significance of this and later transmission lines was that power could be sent in almost any direction between major load centers in the Pacific Northwest, and enabled power users to establish plants distant from the site of power generation.

Since the linking of Grand Coulee and Bonneville, many more dams have been constructed and hundreds of miles of transmission lines have been built. Private and public utilities also participate in the purchase and use of federal power, and contribute their own facilities to the power grid. The result is that the Pacific Northwest enjoys one of the strongest and most flexible power generation and transmission systems in the nation, and the chances of major area power outages, such as have plagued New York City, are few.

Quincy Scott

Ah — Haven't We Met Somewhere?
7 September 1939

The date on this cartoon is important, because it appeared within a week after World War II started in Poland.

Scott clearly foresaw (as, of course, did many others) that war in Europe would mean an industrial boom in the United States, material shortages, and inevitable higher prices for the consumer. This happened, but the full panoply of wartime controls was not instituted until after Pearl Harbor.

Scott's use of the initials "H.C.L." for the high cost of living was nothing new, as the term was widely used during World War I and the boom of the 1920s.

53 *Quincy Scott*

Poland
19 September 1939

The tragic fate of Poland was sealed less than three weeks after the German Wehrmacht struck—and it was sealed with a big assist from Soviet Russia, who grabbed off the eastern half of the country, probably to Hitler's dismay. Without firing a shot, the Soviet Union thus claimed much real estate that it felt historically was Russia's (earned by Tsarist Russia in an earlier partition, and reversed by the creation of a new Poland after World War I). This perfidy on the part of the Soviet Union was duplicated later in World War II, when, after Japan's defeat became a certainty, Russia entered the war on that front and seized Manchuria, northern Korea and the Kurile Islands.

It is true that Hitler and Stalin were nominal allies at the moment of the German invasion of Poland, but the weakness of this alliance was demonstrated June 22, 1941, when Hitler's armies marched in turn against the Soviet Union itself.

Quincy Scott

Mutual Assistance Pacts
10 October 1939

To Stalin no amount of territory under control along the Soviet Union's borders seemed to guarantee security. For this ostensible reason, but also because Stalin coveted their territory, the USSR concluded a series of mutual assistance pacts with the Baltic states in the fall of 1939, after the outbreak of World War II. (This in spite of the fact that the notorious Hitler-Stalin Non-Aggression Pact made the previous summer would appear to give the Soviet Union the assurance it needed that Germany would not attack.)

Of the four states involved, Finland was the most recalcitrant, and that country would not sign the proposed agreement with the Soviets, which would have given the latter the right to purchase the naval base at Hangö, plus other defensive considerations. As a result the Russo-Finnish War broke out in late November, 1939. Finland was defeated after a gallant defense, but managed, however, to retain its independence.

Lithuania, Estonia and Latvia were not so lucky. After the fall of France, the USSR accused them of a conspiracy to aid the Germans, and occupied them after going through the motions of a diplomatic coup. The Soviet occupation lasted only a year, as Germany took the small countries when she attacked Russia in June, 1941. At the end of World War II, victorious Soviet Union reoccupied them for good.

55 *Quincy Scott*

Poor Fox!
21 November 1939

The Russo-Finnish War, which began only a few days after this cartoon appeared, was largely a disaster for the Soviets. Though the Soviet army won at the end of a bitter winter campaign, it had great difficulty in subduing the gallant Finnish troops.

The Finns' resistance achieved a certain success. The Soviets did not occupy the country, but claimed only certain strategic territory that it wanted in the event of war with Germany.

The war had one peculiar angle. The Soviet army's ineptness was claimed by some to have been deliberate on the part of Stalin, to give Hitler a false impression of the combat abilities of the Red army. It is more likely, however, that Stalin miscalculated the ability of the Finns, and failed to use the "blitz" of troops and material that Hitler hurled, for example, against Poland.

A Voice from the Wayside: Carry On!
19 May 1940

Appearing only nine days after German troops crossed into the Low Countries, this cartoon expressed the hope of the anti-fascist world that the French army could duplicate what the "contemptible little army" of 1914 had accomplished—halting the German juggernaut and eventually throwing it back. This did not happen, of course; by early June, the British were evacuating Dunkirk, the Germans were sending armored columns and dive bombers around the north flank of the Maginot Line, and within days all of northern France was overrun.

On June 22, after aging Marshal Petain had issued a call for an armistice, the French signed a harsh armistice in the same railway car at Compiegne in which the World War I armistice had been signed.

57 *Quincy Scott*

Last Ditch
31 May 1940

This cartoon was printed five days before the evacuation of Dunkirk, and it referred to the defense of a beachhead in Belgium by the British, rather than to the Battle of Britain that was to follow.

But in retrospect, the cartoon's subject describes the coming defense of England itself—the great air battles of late summer, the bombing of English cities, preparations for fighting on the island itself ("We will fight them on the beaches,...").

There will always be speculation that if Hitler had jumped off across the English Channel immediately after the fall of France, he could have conquered the British Isles. But, it was an overconfident Goering who felt the battle had to be won first in the skies; whether he was right or wrong, the British won by the scantiest of margins.

Quincy Scott

Tight Traces
12 June 1940

With the fall of France imminent, it became obvious that, if it were not to be caught in the same state of unpreparedness in which Britain and France had found themselves less than a year earlier, the United States would have to redouble its own war preparations.

This was a call for a bipartisan defense effort. Although the "America Firsters" and other isolationists made loud noises during the presidential election of 1940, there was general support for President Roosevelt's preparedness program, including calling the National Guard into federal service in October of that year.

From this point on, political argument was not so much whether to prepare, but what measures would be necessary. Destroyers to Britain, allocation of scarce materials, broadening of the chief executive's powers, establishment of new defense agencies—these were the matters that concerned Americans after the fall of France and the ensuing Battle of Britain.

59 *Quincy Scott*

In the Palace of the Kings of France
14 July 1940

One of the most poignant cartoons ever penned by Scott, and symbolically published on Bastille Day. It shows Marshal Philippe Pétain, hero of Verdun and commander of all French forces in World War I, signing on as chief-of-state of Occupied France under German domination after the French defeat in June, 1940.

Many remember the Vichy government as the fiefdom of Premier Pierre Laval, the official "Quisling" of the French occupation, but it was Pétain who was president, and it was Pétain who gave the occupation the color of legitimacy.

The shadowy figures in the background are marshals Foch, Allied Chief in World War I, Joffre and General Mangin, all leading French military figures in World War I, who of course would have been humiliated to think a French general would prostitute himself to serve the invaders, especially "les sales Boches." Ironically, Pétain's capitulation was a prime reason why the French later took such pride in the feats of General Giraud, who escaped from a German prison camp to serve the Allies, and General de Gaulle, who became the leader of the Free French.

128

"I Shall Not Attend the Convention..."
15 July 1940

Tongue in cheek, Scott illustrated President Roosevelt's suggestion that the 1940 convention was wide open and that he would not attend. But, the poor Democratic donkey was in reality carrying an FDR saddle that could not be shaken. The cartoon merely pictorialized what nobody at the time, including Democrats, would debate—that Roosevelt was going for a third term, damn the consequences.

Roosevelt won an unprecedented third term, and then a fourth. But there were strong feelings among Americans in 1940 that two terms were enough for any chief executive; a feeling that has since been given concrete form in the Twenty-second Amendment (1951).

61

Vista

6 October 1940

This is his opponents' argument against the third term for Roosevelt boiled down to its essentials. Scott and others feared a crown lay at the end of the vista FDR had pictured as his own future. Not a real crown with diamonds and rubies, perhaps, but its equivalent—absolute power at the helm of the world's strongest nation.

It is more likely that Roosevelt, guiding the country through the rapids that preceded the cataract of World War II, honestly believed himself best qualified to act as pilot in those perilous times, and was simply unwilling to turn the helm over to anyone else.

There was much less outcry when Roosevelt announced for a fourth term in 1944 than when he declared for his third. The country was obviously unprepared to switch leaders during the war, and Roosevelt whipped Dewey rather handily in the 1944 election.

132

62 *Quincy Scott*

Vulcan
20 February 1941

This was a salute to the Columbia River defense industries, centered around the Oregon shipyards, on the Willamette River near its juncture with the Columbia at the northwest tip of Portland, and the Kaiser shipyards in Vancouver, Washington. During World War II these yards turned out hundreds of Liberty ships and other craft and employed many thousand workers.

As a result of shipyard activity a housing project called Vanport was constructed near the south end of the Interstate Bridge between Portland and Vancouver. When the war ended, there was much debate about what to do with Vanport, then the second most populous city in Oregon, but the debate was made moot by the flood of Memorial Day, 1948, which destroyed the project.

Another result of the growth of the wartime shipyards was the influx of workers from many parts of the United States, including many Blacks from the South. When the war ended, a high percentage of these workers elected to stay in the Portland area, and as a result Portland gained several thousand Black inhabitants in place of the few dozen families who had lived in the city before the war.

63 *Quincy Scott*

This Is No Practice Hike
22 October 1942

It seems likely that this cartoon was a "pepper-upper" for the war effort, since it did not coincide with any historic turning point in the war. The battle for Guadalcanal in the Pacific had begun two months earlier, and the landings in North Africa were still weeks away.

It is probable that Scott had run across some instances of home-front grumbling, which he could not abide, and decided to tell his readers that they had best cinch up their belts and get on with it. Financing the war effort depended heavily upon the sale of E-bonds, in addition to stepped-up income taxes and taxes on excess profits, and Scott's message — "Highest taxes, biggest war" — was designed to put this need in proper perspective.

64 *Quincy Scott*

Not the First To Pass This Way
23 December 1942

In the second winter of the Russian campaign, Hitler had obviously failed
to achieve his objectives of smashing Soviet resistance and seizing
Moscow. Most of his ranking generals, including the tank expert, Heinz
Guderian, had counseled going into winter quarters and husbanding German strength for a giant offensive in the spring, when the ground would
have hardened sufficiently for tank warfare.

But Hitler, infallible in his own mind, insisted on maintaining a max-
imum offensive effort in the face of bitter winter weather, heavy snowfall
and icebound rivers. The drain on the German army's logistical system
was severe, to say nothing of the campaign's effects on the troops. The
German defeat at Stalingrad, with the loss of Von Paulus' Sixth Army
and some 150,000 men, was only a month away, and it was obvious that
Hitler was about to follow Napoleon in ignominious retreat from
Moscow.

65 *Quincy Scott*

Powder Room
28 April 1943

Stormy describes John L. Lewis, for many years president of the United Mine Workers, and stormy were his relationships with President Roosevelt and other national leaders before, during and after World War II. This cartoon depicts only one in a series of confrontations between Lewis, Roosevelt and the War Labor Board, when Lewis wanted to pull his workers from the coal mines for higher wages.

It is difficult to assess the John L. Lewis of this period. He was fiercely loyal to his miners, and although no one questioned his Americanism, that loyalty often seemed to take precedence over his loyalty to his country. A man of action and not given to the public baring of his inner thoughts, it is likely that he just wanted to get all he could get for his union members while they were helping to fuel the war effort.

140

Quincy Scott

Basic English—(Two Words for the List)
24 November 1943

By late 1943, after the fall of Sicily and the Soviets' seizing the initiative on the eastern front, Hitler and his advisers had begun to cast around for some long-range solution to their problems other than military conquest of the world.

But the Allies, at every opportunity, met Axis feelers by reiterating the terms first laid down at the Casablanca Conference in January, 1943: unconditional surrender.

There have been many editorials and essays on the thesis that the Allies might have saved thousands of lives and shortened the war by many months if they had demanded less stringent terms, allowing some latitude for negotiation. But it is hard to imagine a post-war world in which Hitler and the Nazi party would have been allowed a semblance of legitimacy and a shred of power.

So the Allies plunged on toward destiny and success—the unconditional surrender of the Axis forces.

67 *Quincy Scott*

Music
24 May 1944

The date of this cartoon is especially significant: the middle of three days during which Allied forces were breaking out of the Anzio Beachhead. The music they heard was the advance of the Fifth Army forces from the south, including the spectacular progress of French Moroccan troops through the mountains that bordered the west coast of Italy.

The author included this cartoon partly, if not entirely, because he was on Anzio as assistant intelligence officer of the Third Infantry Division when this was taking place. As part of his duties, he made up an overlay that showed the disposition of German forces and defenses as reported during the previous month by ground patrols, aerial reconnaissance, Italian line-crossers and other sources. This overlay, which went with operations orders to all Third Division troops and attachments taking part in the breakout, gave an accurate and chilling impression of the minefields, wire entanglements, machine gun emplacements and field fortifications, as well as the number, identification and strength of enemy forces.

In spite of this array, the Third Division and other Allied troops broke through the encirclement in three days. The Third Division suffered 995 casualties, killed and wounded, in the first day's action alone, possibly the highest number of battle casualties suffered by any American division in any one day on all fronts in World War II.

144

68 *Quincy Scott*

Historic Pledge Redeemed
11 January 1945

When General Douglas MacArthur left Corregidor for Australia in the spring of 1942, he said, "I shall return."

This is the historic pledge he redeemed when American troops landed in Lingayen Gulf on Luzon January 9, 1945. Manila fell not long afterward, and the Philippines were again free.

The liberation of the Philippines actually began with the invasion of Leyte the preceding October 19. Some journalists hailed this date as the redemption of MacArthur's historic pledge, but Scott apparently chose to wait until the general returned to the island from which he had fled nearly three years earlier.

69 *Quincy Scott*

S'il Vous Plait, Messieurs
21 January 1945

There was nothing tentative about de Gaulle's knocking at the door of the Big Three, and he kept at it until the Three became the Big Four, with France awarded a permanent seat on the Security Council, a veto in the United Nations, a section of Occupied Germany and a position on the Berlin Allied Control Commission.

All this lay in the future; the end of World War II was still nearly seven months away; the formation of the United Nations nearly a year.

One can understand why Roosevelt, Churchill and Stalin regarded de Gaulle as a prickly nuisance, but one can also appreciate what de Gaulle did to rally French resistance and to hasten the defeat of Germany.

70

QuiNcy Scott

"The Ceiling Becomes a Floor"—Sen. Cordon 16 June 1945

The title of this cartoon, attributed to Senator Guy Cordon of Oregon, simply recognizes the economic law that if you attempt to put a price ceiling on a product (in this case, beef) for which demand exceeds supply, the black-market price for the product starts where the legal market stops, and the legal ceiling becomes the floor for the black-market price.

How high above the ceiling the price eventually goes depends on the relative scarcity of the item. If the item is fairly plentiful, the price will not go very high; but it will never sink lower than the legal ceiling, because once it does, people start buying at the same prices on the legal market.

Black marketing was never a truly serious problem in the United States during World War II for two main reasons: First, most citizens were patriotic enough to live by their ration points; second, food was always in fair enough supply that no one was in danger of starvation. Gasoline was a somewhat different matter, but because of the distribution system (metered pumps at the service stations), it was a difficult item to sell illegally.

There were the usual horror stories about bribery and illegal purchasing, but compared to the black marketing in Europe and other areas that suffered a complete absence of some items, Americans were comparatively well off.

71

Quincy Scott

The Fledgling of 169 Years Ago
4 July 1945

In this Fourth of July cartoon, Scott drew what many were thinking—that the United States, whether it sought the honor or not, had been forced into a position of international leadership by the tides of history. Victory in World War II, then a reality in Europe and close to reality in Asia, was only a visible milestone in a situation that had been evolving for decades.

Scott was not, in the deepest sense, an internationalist. His friend Clarence Streit, in his book *Union Now* had argued persuasively for political union of the free nations of the world, but Scott had serious reservations about the wisdom of this course. He was realistic enough to see, however, that America could not abdicate responsibilities without leaving a dangerous vacuum in the world order.

LEADERSHIP AMONG THE NATIONS

QUINCY SCOTT

72

Quincy Scott

The Thinker
8 August 1945

Two days before this cartoon appeared, the United States dropped an atom bomb on Hiroshima. It did not take Quincy Scott long to penetrate the dilemma that the atom bomb posed for humanity: What to do with this awesome new power that the fission of the uranium atom represented?

It is significant that the Thinker—mankind—is looking at the A-bomb here. He is not simply looking at the atom. Thus it is probable that Scott was pondering the military uses of atomic power, rather than peacetime uses like power production.

This is another of his many characterizations that could be published without a caption today, and have equal significance for his readers.

73

Combination
28 December 1945

It is not to be wondered at that every power in the world, including especially England and Russia, would want to know the secret of the atom bomb. Revelations since war's end have let us in on the machinations of spies on both sides.

The U.S., of course, willingly let Britain in on its secrets, and it took the Russians only four years to develop an atom bomb of their own. But there is little question that American monopoly of the bomb in the critical months after World War II helped to solidify the peace.

ATOM SECRET

Quincy Scott

74

To Bell the Cat
30 March 1946

Long and bitter controversy swirled through the United Nations and other international councils concerning the problem of control over atomic power. The United States would not accept any form of control that did not provide for impartial inspection of any nation's atomic facilities; Russia would not accept any form of control that did.

No form of control was adopted, and the only forward steps in the past thirty years have been the non-proliferation pact, to which several key nations (but not all) have adhered, the mutual test ban agreed to by the United States and the Soviet Union, and the SALT I Agreement.

The fairly rapid spread of nuclear technology is rendering the question more and more academic.

75

Open and Shut
30 June 1946

It was typical of many Iron Curtain countries, including in this case Yugoslavia, that they opened their borders to relief supplies from the United Nations Relief and Rehabilitation Agency (UNRRA — Scott made a slight error in his initials), but kept the same borders closed to any information flowing the other way.

In the days before the Marshall Plan, relief activity was extremely important, because the Germans had no compunctions about letting the citizens of occupied countries go without food and clothing.

Wealthy individuals could eat by selling jewelry and heirlooms, a few at a time, and buying food on the black market. But ordinary folk, especially in the cities, had few alternatives to starvation. This situation was normal for the occupied territories during the war, and this was worsened by the disorganization that accompanied the defeat of the Germans. The job faced by UNRRA was indeed a mountainous one.

76

QUINCY SCOTT

On Your Own, John
17 August 1946

Why was John Bull entrusted with the highly treacherous job of trying to work out a solution for the Palestinian question?

While the roots of the problem are buried deep in history, the proximate cause was the Balfour Declaration, a unilateral statement by David Lloyd George's foreign secretary, Lord Balfour, in March, 1916. The statement expressed the British government's "sympathy" with "Jewish Zionist aspirations," and viewed favorably the establishment of a Jewish national homeland in Palestine, with full protection for the rights and property of Palestinian Arabs.

In 1922 the League of Nations followed this up by granting England a mandate to govern Palestine under a temporary administration on behalf of the Jewish people.

Neither the Balfour Declaration nor the League mandate was viewed favorably by the non-Jewish Palestinians. These documents did, however, give the color of legitimacy to Jewish claims on Palestine, and encouraged the Jewish initiative in establishing the state of Israel, with the series of bloody wars that followed.

At the time this cartoon appeared, the English were seeking a way to reconcile the conflicting interests while keeping their own influence in strategic Palestine afloat.

PALESTINE

77

Quincy Scott

Spell You, Old Timer?
25 October 1946

The fledgling United Nations General Assembly here offers to take the burden of the world from the shoulders of Atlas. Would that all the high hopes that were held for the success of the United Nations had come to fruition!

Ahead lay the Cold War, the crises in Hungary and Czechoslovakia, the Berlin airlift, Communist aggression in Korea and the war in Vietnam, the birth of Israel with the four wars that followed, sanctions against Rhodesia and dozens of other international flashpoints. Except for Korea, when the Security Council (following Russia's walkout) authorized concerted action against North Korea, the UN has been relatively helpless to formulate and enforce measures for keeping peace and settling international disputes.

78

QUINCY SCOTT

(Untitled)
26 October 1946

Nearly two years before he entered the lists as an independent candidate for president, Henry Wallace was vainly trying to swing the Democratic party *his* way—that is, farther to the left. Little matter to Henry that a leftward swing at that time would probably have toppled the party off the cliff, since the nation in the immediate postwar years was in a marked conservative trend.

Only a week after this cartoon appeared, the national elections swept Republicans into control of the House of Representatives for the first and only time in two generations, and many freshman senators were Republicans.

This mattered little to Wallace. He was doctrinaire to the point of accepting defeat in preference to compromising his ultra-liberal beliefs, and like Barry Goldwater—on the other side of the fence in 1964—he felt that only by rallying around these beliefs could his party find salvation.

79

Quincy Scott

Happy Days Are Here Again!
21 December 1946

American males never missed two-pants suits until wartime restrictions made them unavailable.

While two-pants suits had been around for many years before World War II, they really came into their own during the depression. They were the result of an inflexible sartorial law: that the pants of a suit always wear out before the jacket does. If you got two pairs of pants with a suit, the jacket could theoretically be worn twice as long.

Lifting the ban on two-pants suits after the war may have been a psychological boost for the men, but it did not do much for the clothing business. With the well-advertised postwar prosperity, and the advent of mix-and-match jackets and slacks, the two-pants suit never again approached its pre-war popularity.

80

Quincy Scott

Wants His Driver's License Extended
5 February 1947

President Truman proposed, eighteen months after World War II ended, that wartime controls, including the allocation of materials, be extended for a transition period. His fear was that immediate decontrol, accompanied by explosive pent-up demand, would start an inflationary spiral.

Congress did not go along with the president, and controls were ended. Prices did go up over a brief period but soon stabilized, as American business began turning out the peacetime goods the nation wanted.

It was just as well. Even in the brief eighteen-month interim, serious distortions were beginning to appear as the old office of Price Administration attempted to keep wartime price levels on virtually everything in the marketplace in the face of demand that would not be denied.

81

Quincy Scott

Carry on, Chaps; I'm Jolly Well Leaving the Act
23 February 1947

England's action in granting India independence ranks with the United States' freeing of the Philippines a few months earlier, one of the few times in history when a great nation has voluntarily given up sovereignty over a weaker nation.

Because of strong ties between Britain and India, the latter has remained a member of the British Commonwealth. Britain has rendered what assistance it could in disputes between India and Pakistan, and in other areas. English is still widely used in India, especially in government and higher education.

82

He Has Joined the Host of Our Legendary Pioneers
9 April 1947

The death of Henry Ford, prototypical Americal industrialist and self-made man, was certainly worth memorializing in a cartoon. A mechanic and engineer by training and experience, Ford built his first automobile in 1893 and founded the Ford Motor Company in 1903.

He was credited with popularization of the assembly line as a manufacturing technique, although he did not invent it. In 1914, he astounded the industrial world by increasing wages from an average of $2.50 per day to $5.00. He successfully did this to prevent the high turnover of labor in his plant, due to the monotony of the work.

From 1908, when the Model T was introduced, until 1927, when it was discontinued for the Model A, Ford turned out approximately fifteen million cars. Nearly all of these were two models, a touring car and a roadster, and all were black. Time and public taste finally caught up with Ford Motor Company; it remains a viable industrial giant today.

83 *Quincy Scott*

Borrowing Neighbors
19 June 1947

This cartoon appeared several years before serious studies of transporting Columbia River water to California began to surface publicly, but already Scott was reflecting the common knowledge that Californians were casting covetous eyes on the enormous water resources of the Pacific Northwest.

Whether or not such a project is ever established, history may render the question moot. As time goes on, and demand for water increases in the Pacific Northwest itself, there may be no way that the export of fresh water to the south can be politically justified. Irrigation of vast tracts of desert land in eastern Washington and Oregon is just one of many demands being made on the Columbia; cooling nuclear plants is another one, and maintenance of salmon habitat a third. The Columbia already furnishes domestic water supplies for several cities, and may furnish more as time goes on.

84

Quincy Scott

Gamely Struggling to Survive
27 June 1947

The controversy of the salmon fishery versus hydroelectric dams is still going on in the Pacific Northwest, although the argument is now largely academic since the dams are already built at most of the good sites. While millions of dollars have been spent on fishways, research, additional hatchery facilities, and trucking adult salmon around high dams, no one argues the fact that the salmon fishery has been greatly damaged.

Dams, to be sure, have not been the sole culprits. Heavy pressure by commercial and sport fishermen, destruction of spawning grounds, and pollution of streams have contributed to the decline of the salmon. But dams bear much of the responsibility. The turbines have caused the death of sea-bound fingerlings, and adult fish die in the nitrogen-saturated waters at the foot of the spillways. (High counts of salmon moving upstream at the Bonneville counting station do not necessarily prove that the escapement is as great as it would be if the dam were not there.)

Scott was not taking a position in this cartoon. He was simply saying that if the Northwest continued to build dams for needed hydroelectric power, it would be difficult for the valuable salmon fishery to survive.

85

Quincy Scott

Another Lost-Boy Hunt
16 July 1947

This is one of the more apt of Quincy Scott portrayals of political shenanigans. Although Wayne Morse had been elected senator from Oregon on the Republican ticket only three years earlier, Senate Republicans were already having problems keeping track of their maverick cohort. This was five years before Morse split from the GOP and moved his chair to the center aisle of the Senate as an independent, and six years before he went all the way and declared as a Democrat.

There is not room in this brief space to record all of Wayne Morse's reversals of position, but there was a saying current in Oregon when Morse was ill that "something he agreed with is eating him." Whenever a Senate vote was recorded as 95 to 1, one could be fairly sure that the single negative vote was Morse's. He was one of two senators who voted against the Gulf of Tonkin Resolution, and was a lonely minority of one on many occasions.

86 *Quincy Scott*

Resignation of Eduard Benes
9 June 1948

Czechoslovakia was one of the East European states upon which Russia wished to put its stamp of authority following World War II, and Eduard Benes was the unfortunate individual who happened to occupy the presidential chair when the Communist coup occurred in June, 1948. Although the coup was ostensibly engineered by the Czech Communist Party, there is little doubt that it had the complete backing and military muscle of the Soviet Union.

Benes escaped the fate of Jan Masaryk, who is believed to have been murdered by the Communists (although his death was announced as a suicide), but Benes died, a broken man, only three months after his resignation.

Benes deserved better of history, having had a distinguished career between World War I and World War II, serving as foreign minister, prime minister and president of Czechoslovakia. He was a prominent figure at the League of Nations and was outspoken on the subjects of human rights and the need for democratic institutions. But he stood in the Soviet Union's way at the wrong moment.

87 Quincy Scott

"—Once in the Saddle—"
3 July 1948

One has difficulty in recalling that Harry Truman was in strong disfavor with Democratic party chieftains prior to the 1948 convention. He had taken three major steps in domestic affairs that brought about this dissension: he tried to continue wartime controls; he had tried to reactivate many unpopular New Deal programs; and he had vetoed the Taft-Hartley Act, a veto that Congress overturned.

Add to this the fact that such party leaders as Jimmy Byrnes and Herbert Lehman felt they had stronger claims to the presidential nomination than did Truman. So in spite of his successes in foreign affairs—the Truman Doctrine and the Marshall Plan—he approached the convention facing some powerful opposition.

But as Scott noted, "You can't say no to the incumbent," and this political truism was repeated at the Democratic convention. They did not say no to Truman, and he went on to win the election.

88 *Quincy Scott*

Henry's Henry
25 July 1948

Henry A. Wallace, a controversial and quixotic figure in American
politics, is thought to have entered the 1948 presidential race as a third-
party candidate for two reasons: he was tremendously miffed at President
Roosevelt's failure to keep him on as vice president in the 1944 campaign,
choosing Harry Truman instead; and Wallace also believed that he was
the best man suited to lead the nation in the postwar years.

Although some would expect a man with Wallace's Iowa background
to be strongly conservative, the reverse was true. He was visionary, a
believer in the power of the government to do whatever was necessary for
the good of the people, and a man who often let his radical principles
overcome the dictates of sound politics.

Not only was Wallace soundly beaten in the 1948 general election, but
he even failed to prevent Truman from winning the election, which was
doubtless Wallace's secondary goal.

89

Quincy Scott

Come as Early and Stay as Late as You Can
8 September 1947

This is one of the cartoons that clearly shows Scott's delight with the fine weather that can occur at almost any time in western Oregon. On such days in the late spring and early fall temperatures are characteristically in the 80s, with low humidity and little wind. Such periods occur when the Portland area is under the influence of the "Pacific high," with the storm track well to the eastward, and several days of near-perfect weather in succession can be expected.

Scott may have jumped the gun a bit with this cartoon, since the date indicates that autumn proper was still two weeks away. There are also many definitions of what "Indian summer" really means, most purists contending that it is a period of unseasonably warm weather in the late fall.

90

Quincy Scott

Birdie, Make 'Em Quit Pickin' on Me!
30 October 1948

Josef Stalin could not understand why the Dove of Peace would not leave him alone. He thought that because of his superior military strength ("How many divisions does the Pope have?") he could take unilateral action of any kind without other powers countering his moves.

Thus, when he put the Berlin blockade into effect in 1948, he expected the United States, Britain and France to give in meekly and get out of West Berlin. He did not reckon with the resolve of the United States and its president, Harry S. Truman. The Berlin airlift, which Stalin did not dare interrupt by military action, succeeded in carrying more than 1,500,000 tons of supplies to the beleaguered city before the blockade was lifted in May, 1949.

INDEX

[Figures refer to cartoon numbers]
[Bold face page numbers index the introductory matter]

192

194

196